SAMUEL BARBER
Horizon

Full Score

Edited by David Flachs

First Edition

ED 4463
First Printing: November 2010

ISBN 978-1-4234-9980-0

G. SCHIRMER, Inc.

DISTRIBUTED BY

HAL•LEONARD®
CORPORATION
7777 W. BLUEMOUND RD. P.O. BOX 13819 MILWAUKEE, WI 53213

www.schirmer.com
www.halleonard.com

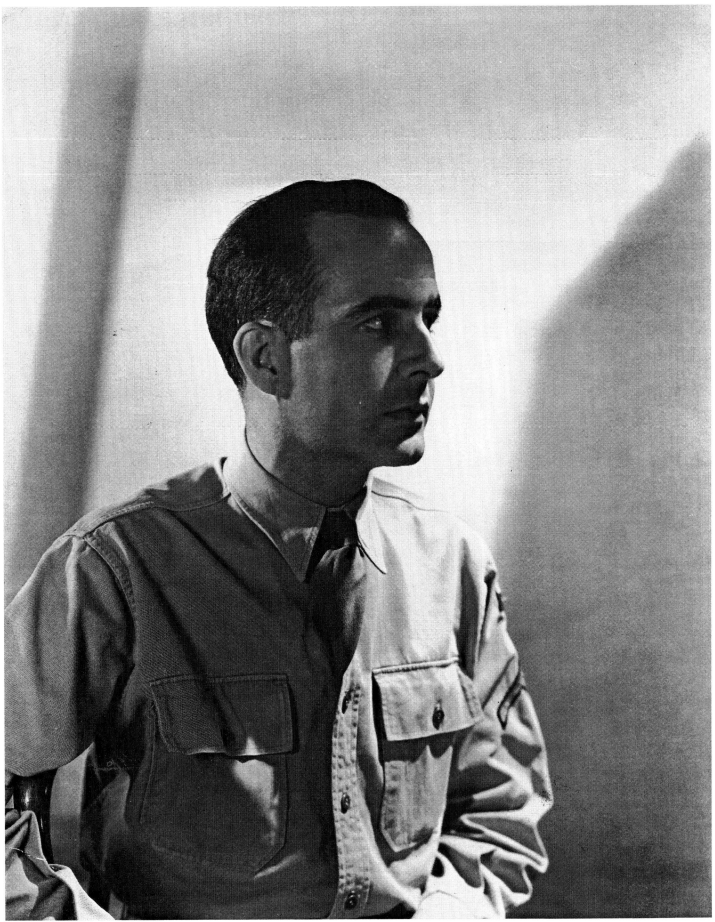

Early photo of Samuel Barber in Army uniform, 1940s.

Horizon is one of Barber's few orchestral works which remained unpublished during his lifetime. The little that is known about this work can be attributed to the research and writings of Barbara Heyman.

Horizon was composed in 1945 when Barber was writing music for radio broadcasts sponsored by the United States Office of War Information. The first performance was on 17 June 1945 on the NBC radio broadcast, "The Standard Oil Hour," by the San Francisco Symphony, under the direction of Efrem Kurtz.

Barber later drew on the opening measures of *Horizon*, for *Summer Music* (1956) his only woodwind quintet, which was commissioned by the Chamber Music Society of Detroit.

The first commercial recording of *Horizon* was made by the San Diego Chamber Orchestra under the direction of Donald Barra. The recording was distributed through Koch International Classics.

Horizon is catalogued as "H-111" in Barbara Heyman's *Samuel Barber: A Thematic Catalogue of the Complete Works.*

Instrumentation

Flute
2 Oboes
2 Clarinets in B flat
2 Bassoons
2 Horns in F
Trumpet in C
Timpani
Harp
Strings

duration ca. 5 minutes

Performance material is available on rental from the publisher.
G. Schirmer/AMP Rental and Performance Department
P.O. Box 572
445 Bellvale Road
Chester, NY 10918
(845) 469-4699 - phone
(845) 469-7544 - fax
www.schirmer.com

HORIZON

Samuel Barber